Nightly

Self Reflection
Journal

Copyright © 2022

Take 10-15 minutes each night to reflect on your day and write down your thoughts on the two pages. By repeating the affirmation out loud at the end of your reflecting, you're helping to clear and calm your mind. This also helps prepare for a great night's sleep and a positive next morning. You'll be surprised by how much progress you've made after 90 days. Consistency, effort, and good intention is key. You've got this!

-Brooke

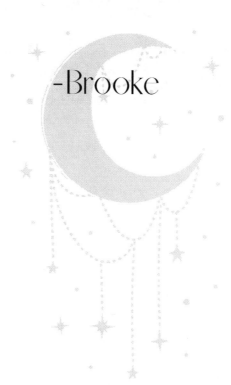

Nightly

Self Reflection
Journal

This Journal belongs to:

_____

MY NIGHTLY
REFLECTION PROMPTS

READ THE PROMPTS BELOW AND RESPOND BY
FILLING IN EACH SPACE WITH IMAGES OR WORDS
THAT COME TO MIND.

The best things that
happened today:

Things I wish I could
change about today:

I am proud of myself
today because...

I think I still need
to work on...

MY NIGHTLY
REFLECTION PROMPTS

READ THE PROMPTS BELOW AND RESPOND BY FILLING IN
EACH SPACE WITH IMAGES OR WORDS THAT COME TO
MIND. LASTLY, REPEAT THE AFFIRMATION AT THE
BOTTOM OF THE PAGE OUT LOUD 3 TIMES.

My overall mood today:

calm	confident	nervous
happy	angry	grateful
sad	jealous	curious

Any others that came up:

My overall rating of the day:

1   2   3   4   5   6   7   8   9   10

Any and all other thoughts:

I RELEASE THIS DAY AND CALL BACK MY PEACE, POWER, AND POSITIVE ENERGY!

MY NIGHTLY REFLECTION PROMPTS

READ THE PROMPTS BELOW AND RESPOND BY
FILLING IN EACH SPACE WITH IMAGES OR WORDS
THAT COME TO MIND.

The best things that
happened today:

Things I wish I could
change about today:

I am proud of myself
today because...

I think I still need
to work on...

MY NIGHTLY
REFLECTION PROMPTS

READ THE PROMPTS BELOW AND RESPOND BY FILLING IN
EACH SPACE WITH IMAGES OR WORDS THAT COME TO
MIND. LASTLY, REPEAT THE AFFIRMATION AT THE
BOTTOM OF THE PAGE OUT LOUD 3 TIMES.

My overall mood today:

calm	confident	nervous
happy	angry	grateful
sad	jealous	curious

Any others that came up:

My overall rating of the day:

1   2   3   4   5   6   7   8   9   10

Any and all other thoughts:

I RELEASE THIS DAY AND CALL BACK MY PEACE, POWER, AND POSITIVE ENERGY!

MY NIGHTLY REFLECTION PROMPTS

READ THE PROMPTS BELOW AND RESPOND BY
FILLING IN EACH SPACE WITH IMAGES OR WORDS
THAT COME TO MIND.

The best things that
happened today:

Things I wish I could
change about today:

I am proud of myself
today because...

I think I still need
to work on...

MY NIGHTLY
REFLECTION PROMPTS

READ THE PROMPTS BELOW AND RESPOND BY FILLING IN
EACH SPACE WITH IMAGES OR WORDS THAT COME TO
MIND. LASTLY, REPEAT THE AFFIRMATION AT THE
BOTTOM OF THE PAGE OUT LOUD 3 TIMES.

My overall mood today:

calm	confident	nervous
happy	angry	grateful
sad	jealous	curious

Any others that came up:

My overall rating of the day:

1   2   3   4   5   6   7   8   9   10

Any and all other thoughts:

I RELEASE THIS DAY AND CALL BACK MY PEACE, POWER, AND POSITIVE ENERGY!

MY NIGHTLY REFLECTION PROMPTS

READ THE PROMPTS BELOW AND RESPOND BY
FILLING IN EACH SPACE WITH IMAGES OR WORDS
THAT COME TO MIND.

The best things that
happened today:

Things I wish I could
change about today:

I am proud of myself
today because...

I think I still need
to work on...

MY NIGHTLY
REFLECTION PROMPTS

READ THE PROMPTS BELOW AND RESPOND BY FILLING IN
EACH SPACE WITH IMAGES OR WORDS THAT COME TO
MIND. LASTLY, REPEAT THE AFFIRMATION AT THE
BOTTOM OF THE PAGE OUT LOUD 3 TIMES.

My overall mood today:

calm   confident   nervous

happy   angry   grateful

sad   jealous   curious

Any others that came up:

My overall rating of the day:

1   2   3   4   5   6   7   8   9   10

Any and all other thoughts:

I RELEASE THIS DAY AND CALL BACK MY PEACE, POWER, AND POSITIVE ENERGY!

MY NIGHTLY
REFLECTION PROMPTS

READ THE PROMPTS BELOW AND RESPOND BY
FILLING IN EACH SPACE WITH IMAGES OR WORDS
THAT COME TO MIND.

The best things that
happened today:

Things I wish I could
change about today:

I am proud of myself
today because...

I think I still need
to work on...

MY NIGHTLY
REFLECTION PROMPTS

READ THE PROMPTS BELOW AND RESPOND BY FILLING IN
EACH SPACE WITH IMAGES OR WORDS THAT COME TO
MIND. LASTLY, REPEAT THE AFFIRMATION AT THE
BOTTOM OF THE PAGE OUT LOUD 3 TIMES.

My overall mood today:

calm	confident	nervous
happy	angry	grateful
sad	jealous	curious

Any others that came up:

My overall rating of the day:

1   2   3   4   5   6   7   8   9   10

Any and all other thoughts:

I RELEASE THIS DAY AND CALL BACK MY PEACE, POWER, AND POSITIVE ENERGY!

MY NIGHTLY
REFLECTION PROMPTS

READ THE PROMPTS BELOW AND RESPOND BY
FILLING IN EACH SPACE WITH IMAGES OR WORDS
THAT COME TO MIND.

The best things that
happened today:

Things I wish I could
change about today:

I am proud of myself
today because...

I think I still need
to work on...

MY NIGHTLY
REFLECTION PROMPTS

READ THE PROMPTS BELOW AND RESPOND BY FILLING IN
EACH SPACE WITH IMAGES OR WORDS THAT COME TO
MIND. LASTLY, REPEAT THE AFFIRMATION AT THE
BOTTOM OF THE PAGE OUT LOUD 3 TIMES.

My overall mood today:

calm	confident	nervous
happy	angry	grateful
sad	jealous	curious

Any others that came up:

My overall rating of the day:

1   2   3   4   5   6   7   8   9   10

Any and all other thoughts:

I RELEASE THIS DAY AND CALL BACK MY PEACE, POWER, AND POSITIVE ENERGY!

MY NIGHTLY REFLECTION PROMPTS

READ THE PROMPTS BELOW AND RESPOND BY
FILLING IN EACH SPACE WITH IMAGES OR WORDS
THAT COME TO MIND.

The best things that
happened today:

Things I wish I could
change about today:

I am proud of myself
today because...

I think I still need
to work on...

MY NIGHTLY
REFLECTION PROMPTS

READ THE PROMPTS BELOW AND RESPOND BY FILLING IN
EACH SPACE WITH IMAGES OR WORDS THAT COME TO
MIND. LASTLY, REPEAT THE AFFIRMATION AT THE
BOTTOM OF THE PAGE OUT LOUD 3 TIMES.

My overall mood today:

calm   confident   nervous

happy   angry   grateful

sad   jealous   curious

Any others that came up:

My overall rating of the day:

1   2   3   4   5   6   7   8   9   10

Any and all other thoughts:

I RELEASE THIS DAY AND CALL BACK MY PEACE, POWER, AND POSITIVE ENERGY!

MY NIGHTLY
REFLECTION PROMPTS

READ THE PROMPTS BELOW AND RESPOND BY
FILLING IN EACH SPACE WITH IMAGES OR WORDS
THAT COME TO MIND.

The best things that
happened today:

Things I wish I could
change about today:

I am proud of myself
today because...

I think I still need
to work on...

MY NIGHTLY
REFLECTION PROMPTS

READ THE PROMPTS BELOW AND RESPOND BY FILLING IN
EACH SPACE WITH IMAGES OR WORDS THAT COME TO
MIND. LASTLY, REPEAT THE AFFIRMATION AT THE
BOTTOM OF THE PAGE OUT LOUD 3 TIMES.

My overall mood today:

calm	confident	nervous
happy	angry	grateful
sad	jealous	curious

Any others that came up:

My overall rating of the day:

1   2   3   4   5   6   7   8   9   10

Any and all other thoughts:

I RELEASE THIS DAY AND CALL BACK MY PEACE, POWER, AND POSITIVE ENERGY!

MY NIGHTLY
REFLECTION PROMPTS

READ THE PROMPTS BELOW AND RESPOND BY
FILLING IN EACH SPACE WITH IMAGES OR WORDS
THAT COME TO MIND.

The best things that
happened today:

Things I wish I could
change about today:

I am proud of myself
today because...

I think I still need
to work on...

MY NIGHTLY
REFLECTION PROMPTS

READ THE PROMPTS BELOW AND RESPOND BY FILLING IN
EACH SPACE WITH IMAGES OR WORDS THAT COME TO
MIND. LASTLY, REPEAT THE AFFIRMATION AT THE
BOTTOM OF THE PAGE OUT LOUD 3 TIMES.

My overall mood today:

calm	confident	nervous
happy	angry	grateful
sad	jealous	curious

Any others that came up:

My overall rating of the day:

1   2   3   4   5   6   7   8   9   10

Any and all other thoughts:

I RELEASE THIS DAY AND CALL BACK MY PEACE, POWER, AND POSITIVE ENERGY!

MY NIGHTLY
REFLECTION PROMPTS

READ THE PROMPTS BELOW AND RESPOND BY
FILLING IN EACH SPACE WITH IMAGES OR WORDS
THAT COME TO MIND.

The best things that
happened today:

Things I wish I could
change about today:

I am proud of myself
today because...

I think I still need
to work on...

MY NIGHTLY REFLECTION PROMPTS

READ THE PROMPTS BELOW AND RESPOND BY FILLING IN
EACH SPACE WITH IMAGES OR WORDS THAT COME TO
MIND. LASTLY, REPEAT THE AFFIRMATION AT THE
BOTTOM OF THE PAGE OUT LOUD 3 TIMES.

My overall mood today:

calm	confident	nervous
happy	angry	grateful
sad	jealous	curious

Any others that came up:

My overall rating of the day:

1   2   3   4   5   6   7   8   9   10

Any and all other thoughts:

I RELEASE THIS DAY AND CALL BACK MY PEACE, POWER, AND POSITIVE ENERGY!

MY NIGHTLY
REFLECTION PROMPTS

READ THE PROMPTS BELOW AND RESPOND BY
FILLING IN EACH SPACE WITH IMAGES OR WORDS
THAT COME TO MIND.

The best things that
happened today:

Things I wish I could
change about today:

I am proud of myself
today because...

I think I still need
to work on...

MY NIGHTLY
REFLECTION PROMPTS

READ THE PROMPTS BELOW AND RESPOND BY FILLING IN
EACH SPACE WITH IMAGES OR WORDS THAT COME TO
MIND. LASTLY, REPEAT THE AFFIRMATION AT THE
BOTTOM OF THE PAGE OUT LOUD 3 TIMES.

My overall mood today:

calm   confident   nervous

happy   angry   grateful

sad   jealous   curious

Any others that came up:

My overall rating of the day:

1   2   3   4   5   6   7   8   9   10

Any and all other thoughts:

I RELEASE THIS DAY AND CALL BACK MY PEACE, POWER, AND POSITIVE ENERGY!

MY NIGHTLY
REFLECTION PROMPTS

READ THE PROMPTS BELOW AND RESPOND BY
FILLING IN EACH SPACE WITH IMAGES OR WORDS
THAT COME TO MIND.

The best things that
happened today:

Things I wish I could
change about today:

I am proud of myself
today because...

I think I still need
to work on...

MY NIGHTLY
REFLECTION PROMPTS

READ THE PROMPTS BELOW AND RESPOND BY FILLING IN
EACH SPACE WITH IMAGES OR WORDS THAT COME TO
MIND. LASTLY, REPEAT THE AFFIRMATION AT THE
BOTTOM OF THE PAGE OUT LOUD 3 TIMES.

My overall mood today:

calm	confident	nervous
happy	angry	grateful
sad	jealous	curious

Any others that came up:

My overall rating of the day:

1   2   3   4   5   6   7   8   9   10

Any and all other thoughts:

I RELEASE THIS DAY AND CALL BACK MY PEACE, POWER, AND POSITIVE ENERGY!

MY NIGHTLY REFLECTION PROMPTS

READ THE PROMPTS BELOW AND RESPOND BY
FILLING IN EACH SPACE WITH IMAGES OR WORDS
THAT COME TO MIND.

The best things that
happened today:

Things I wish I could
change about today:

I am proud of myself
today because...

I think I still need
to work on...

MY NIGHTLY
REFLECTION PROMPTS

READ THE PROMPTS BELOW AND RESPOND BY FILLING IN
EACH SPACE WITH IMAGES OR WORDS THAT COME TO
MIND. LASTLY, REPEAT THE AFFIRMATION AT THE
BOTTOM OF THE PAGE OUT LOUD 3 TIMES.

My overall mood today:

calm   confident   nervous

happy   angry   grateful

sad   jealous   curious

Any others that came up:

My overall rating of the day:

1   2   3   4   5   6   7   8   9   10

Any and all other thoughts:

I RELEASE THIS DAY AND CALL BACK MY PEACE, POWER, AND POSITIVE ENERGY!

MY NIGHTLY
REFLECTION PROMPTS

READ THE PROMPTS BELOW AND RESPOND BY
FILLING IN EACH SPACE WITH IMAGES OR WORDS
THAT COME TO MIND.

The best things that
happened today:

Things I wish I could
change about today:

I am proud of myself
today because...

I think I still need
to work on...

MY NIGHTLY
REFLECTION PROMPTS

READ THE PROMPTS BELOW AND RESPOND BY FILLING IN
EACH SPACE WITH IMAGES OR WORDS THAT COME TO
MIND. LASTLY, REPEAT THE AFFIRMATION AT THE
BOTTOM OF THE PAGE OUT LOUD 3 TIMES.

My overall mood today:

calm   confident   nervous

happy   angry   grateful

sad   jealous   curious

Any others that came up:

My overall rating of the day:

1   2   3   4   5   6   7   8   9   10

Any and all other thoughts:

I RELEASE THIS DAY AND CALL BACK MY PEACE, POWER, AND POSITIVE ENERGY!

MY NIGHTLY
REFLECTION PROMPTS

READ THE PROMPTS BELOW AND RESPOND BY
FILLING IN EACH SPACE WITH IMAGES OR WORDS
THAT COME TO MIND.

The best things that
happened today:

Things I wish I could
change about today:

I am proud of myself
today because...

I think I still need
to work on...

MY NIGHTLY
REFLECTION PROMPTS

READ THE PROMPTS BELOW AND RESPOND BY FILLING IN
EACH SPACE WITH IMAGES OR WORDS THAT COME TO
MIND. LASTLY, REPEAT THE AFFIRMATION AT THE
BOTTOM OF THE PAGE OUT LOUD 3 TIMES.

My overall mood today:

calm	confident	nervous
happy	angry	grateful
sad	jealous	curious

Any others that came up:

My overall rating of the day:

1 2 3 4 5 6 7 8 9 10

Any and all other thoughts:

I RELEASE THIS DAY AND CALL BACK MY PEACE, POWER, AND POSITIVE ENERGY!

MY NIGHTLY
REFLECTION PROMPTS

READ THE PROMPTS BELOW AND RESPOND BY
FILLING IN EACH SPACE WITH IMAGES OR WORDS
THAT COME TO MIND.

The best things that
happened today:

Things I wish I could
change about today:

I am proud of myself
today because...

I think I still need
to work on...

MY NIGHTLY
REFLECTION PROMPTS

READ THE PROMPTS BELOW AND RESPOND BY FILLING IN
EACH SPACE WITH IMAGES OR WORDS THAT COME TO
MIND. LASTLY, REPEAT THE AFFIRMATION AT THE
BOTTOM OF THE PAGE OUT LOUD 3 TIMES.

My overall mood today:

calm	confident	nervous
happy	angry	grateful
sad	jealous	curious

Any others that came up:

My overall rating of the day:

1   2   3   4   5   6   7   8   9   10

Any and all other thoughts:

I RELEASE THIS DAY AND CALL BACK MY PEACE, POWER, AND POSITIVE ENERGY!

MY NIGHTLY
REFLECTION PROMPTS

READ THE PROMPTS BELOW AND RESPOND BY
FILLING IN EACH SPACE WITH IMAGES OR WORDS
THAT COME TO MIND.

The best things that
happened today:

Things I wish I could
change about today:

I am proud of myself
today because...

I think I still need
to work on...

MY NIGHTLY REFLECTION PROMPTS

READ THE PROMPTS BELOW AND RESPOND BY FILLING IN
EACH SPACE WITH IMAGES OR WORDS THAT COME TO
MIND. LASTLY, REPEAT THE AFFIRMATION AT THE
BOTTOM OF THE PAGE OUT LOUD 3 TIMES.

My overall mood today:

calm   confident   nervous

happy   angry   grateful

sad   jealous   curious

Any others that came up:

My overall rating of the day:

1   2   3   4   5   6   7   8   9   10

Any and all other thoughts:

I RELEASE THIS DAY AND CALL BACK MY PEACE, POWER, AND POSITIVE ENERGY!

MY NIGHTLY
REFLECTION PROMPTS

READ THE PROMPTS BELOW AND RESPOND BY
FILLING IN EACH SPACE WITH IMAGES OR WORDS
THAT COME TO MIND.

The best things that
happened today:

Things I wish I could
change about today:

I am proud of myself
today because...

I think I still need
to work on...

MY NIGHTLY
REFLECTION PROMPTS

READ THE PROMPTS BELOW AND RESPOND BY FILLING IN
EACH SPACE WITH IMAGES OR WORDS THAT COME TO
MIND. LASTLY, REPEAT THE AFFIRMATION AT THE
BOTTOM OF THE PAGE OUT LOUD 3 TIMES.

My overall mood today:

calm	confident	nervous
happy	angry	grateful
sad	jealous	curious

Any others that came up:

My overall rating of the day:

1 2 3 4 5 6 7 8 9 10

Any and all other thoughts:

I RELEASE THIS DAY AND CALL BACK MY PEACE, POWER, AND POSITIVE ENERGY!

MY NIGHTLY
REFLECTION PROMPTS

READ THE PROMPTS BELOW AND RESPOND BY
FILLING IN EACH SPACE WITH IMAGES OR WORDS
THAT COME TO MIND.

The best things that
happened today:

Things I wish I could
change about today:

I am proud of myself
today because...

I think I still need
to work on...

MY NIGHTLY REFLECTION PROMPTS

READ THE PROMPTS BELOW AND RESPOND BY FILLING IN
EACH SPACE WITH IMAGES OR WORDS THAT COME TO
MIND. LASTLY, REPEAT THE AFFIRMATION AT THE
BOTTOM OF THE PAGE OUT LOUD 3 TIMES.

My overall mood today:

calm   confident   nervous

happy   angry   grateful

sad   jealous   curious

Any others that came up:

My overall rating of the day:

1   2   3   4   5   6   7   8   9   10

Any and all other thoughts:

I RELEASE THIS DAY AND CALL BACK MY PEACE, POWER, AND POSITIVE ENERGY!

MY NIGHTLY
REFLECTION PROMPTS

READ THE PROMPTS BELOW AND RESPOND BY
FILLING IN EACH SPACE WITH IMAGES OR WORDS
THAT COME TO MIND.

The best things that
happened today:

Things I wish I could
change about today:

I am proud of myself
today because...

I think I still need
to work on...

MY NIGHTLY
REFLECTION PROMPTS

READ THE PROMPTS BELOW AND RESPOND BY FILLING IN
EACH SPACE WITH IMAGES OR WORDS THAT COME TO
MIND. LASTLY, REPEAT THE AFFIRMATION AT THE
BOTTOM OF THE PAGE OUT LOUD 3 TIMES.

My overall mood today:

calm   confident   nervous

happy   angry   grateful

sad   jealous   curious

Any others that came up:

My overall rating of the day:

1   2   3   4   5   6   7   8   9   10

Any and all other thoughts:

I RELEASE THIS DAY AND CALL BACK MY PEACE, POWER, AND POSITIVE ENERGY!

MY NIGHTLY
REFLECTION PROMPTS

READ THE PROMPTS BELOW AND RESPOND BY
FILLING IN EACH SPACE WITH IMAGES OR WORDS
THAT COME TO MIND.

The best things that
happened today:

Things I wish I could
change about today:

I am proud of myself
today because...

I think I still need
to work on...

MY NIGHTLY
REFLECTION PROMPTS

READ THE PROMPTS BELOW AND RESPOND BY FILLING IN
EACH SPACE WITH IMAGES OR WORDS THAT COME TO
MIND. LASTLY, REPEAT THE AFFIRMATION AT THE
BOTTOM OF THE PAGE OUT LOUD 3 TIMES.

My overall mood today:

calm	confident	nervous
happy	angry	grateful
sad	jealous	curious

Any others that came up:

My overall rating of the day:

1   2   3   4   5   6   7   8   9   10

Any and all other thoughts:

I RELEASE THIS DAY AND CALL BACK MY PEACE, POWER, AND POSITIVE ENERGY!

MY NIGHTLY REFLECTION PROMPTS

READ THE PROMPTS BELOW AND RESPOND BY
FILLING IN EACH SPACE WITH IMAGES OR WORDS
THAT COME TO MIND.

The best things that
happened today:

Things I wish I could
change about today:

I am proud of myself
today because...

I think I still need
to work on...

MY NIGHTLY
REFLECTION PROMPTS

READ THE PROMPTS BELOW AND RESPOND BY FILLING IN
EACH SPACE WITH IMAGES OR WORDS THAT COME TO
MIND. LASTLY, REPEAT THE AFFIRMATION AT THE
BOTTOM OF THE PAGE OUT LOUD 3 TIMES.

My overall mood today:

calm	confident	nervous
happy	angry	grateful
sad	jealous	curious

Any others that came up:

My overall rating of the day:

1   2   3   4   5   6   7   8   9   10

Any and all other thoughts:

I RELEASE THIS DAY AND CALL BACK MY PEACE, POWER, AND POSITIVE ENERGY!

MY NIGHTLY
REFLECTION PROMPTS

READ THE PROMPTS BELOW AND RESPOND BY
FILLING IN EACH SPACE WITH IMAGES OR WORDS
THAT COME TO MIND.

The best things that
happened today:

Things I wish I could
change about today:

I am proud of myself
today because...

I think I still need
to work on...

MY NIGHTLY
REFLECTION PROMPTS

READ THE PROMPTS BELOW AND RESPOND BY FILLING IN
EACH SPACE WITH IMAGES OR WORDS THAT COME TO
MIND. LASTLY, REPEAT THE AFFIRMATION AT THE
BOTTOM OF THE PAGE OUT LOUD 3 TIMES.

My overall mood today:

calm	confident	nervous
happy	angry	grateful
sad	jealous	curious

Any others that came up:

My overall rating of the day:

1   2   3   4   5   6   7   8   9   10

Any and all other thoughts:

I RELEASE THIS DAY AND CALL BACK MY PEACE, POWER, AND POSITIVE ENERGY!

MY NIGHTLY
REFLECTION PROMPTS

READ THE PROMPTS BELOW AND RESPOND BY
FILLING IN EACH SPACE WITH IMAGES OR WORDS
THAT COME TO MIND.

The best things that
happened today:

Things I wish I could
change about today:

I am proud of myself
today because...

I think I still need
to work on...

MY NIGHTLY
REFLECTION PROMPTS

READ THE PROMPTS BELOW AND RESPOND BY FILLING IN
EACH SPACE WITH IMAGES OR WORDS THAT COME TO
MIND. LASTLY, REPEAT THE AFFIRMATION AT THE
BOTTOM OF THE PAGE OUT LOUD 3 TIMES.

My overall mood today:

calm   confident   nervous

happy   angry   grateful

sad   jealous   curious

Any others that came up:

My overall rating of the day:

1   2   3   4   5   6   7   8   9   10

Any and all other thoughts:

I RELEASE THIS DAY AND CALL BACK MY PEACE, POWER, AND POSITIVE ENERGY!

MY NIGHTLY
REFLECTION PROMPTS

READ THE PROMPTS BELOW AND RESPOND BY
FILLING IN EACH SPACE WITH IMAGES OR WORDS
THAT COME TO MIND.

The best things that
happened today:

Things I wish I could
change about today:

I am proud of myself
today because...

I think I still need
to work on...

MY NIGHTLY REFLECTION PROMPTS

READ THE PROMPTS BELOW AND RESPOND BY FILLING IN EACH SPACE WITH IMAGES OR WORDS THAT COME TO MIND. LASTLY, REPEAT THE AFFIRMATION AT THE BOTTOM OF THE PAGE OUT LOUD 3 TIMES.

My overall mood today:

calm	confident	nervous
happy	angry	grateful
sad	jealous	curious

Any others that came up:

My overall rating of the day:

1   2   3   4   5   6   7   8   9   10

Any and all other thoughts:

I RELEASE THIS DAY AND CALL BACK MY PEACE, POWER, AND POSITIVE ENERGY!

MY NIGHTLY
REFLECTION PROMPTS

READ THE PROMPTS BELOW AND RESPOND BY
FILLING IN EACH SPACE WITH IMAGES OR WORDS
THAT COME TO MIND.

The best things that
happened today:

Things I wish I could
change about today:

I am proud of myself
today because...

I think I still need
to work on...

MY NIGHTLY
REFLECTION PROMPTS

READ THE PROMPTS BELOW AND RESPOND BY FILLING IN
EACH SPACE WITH IMAGES OR WORDS THAT COME TO
MIND. LASTLY, REPEAT THE AFFIRMATION AT THE
BOTTOM OF THE PAGE OUT LOUD 3 TIMES.

My overall mood today:

calm	confident	nervous
happy	angry	grateful
sad	jealous	curious

Any others that came up:

My overall rating of the day:

1   2   3   4   5   6   7   8   9   10

Any and all other thoughts:

I RELEASE THIS DAY AND CALL BACK MY PEACE, POWER, AND POSITIVE ENERGY!

MY NIGHTLY
REFLECTION PROMPTS

READ THE PROMPTS BELOW AND RESPOND BY
FILLING IN EACH SPACE WITH IMAGES OR WORDS
THAT COME TO MIND.

The best things that
happened today:

Things I wish I could
change about today:

I am proud of myself
today because...

I think I still need
to work on...

MY NIGHTLY REFLECTION PROMPTS

READ THE PROMPTS BELOW AND RESPOND BY FILLING IN
EACH SPACE WITH IMAGES OR WORDS THAT COME TO
MIND. LASTLY, REPEAT THE AFFIRMATION AT THE
BOTTOM OF THE PAGE OUT LOUD 3 TIMES.

My overall mood today:

calm   confident   nervous

happy   angry   grateful

sad   jealous   curious

Any others that came up:

My overall rating of the day:

1   2   3   4   5   6   7   8   9   10

Any and all other thoughts:

I RELEASE THIS DAY AND CALL BACK MY PEACE, POWER, AND POSITIVE ENERGY!

MY NIGHTLY
REFLECTION PROMPTS

READ THE PROMPTS BELOW AND RESPOND BY
FILLING IN EACH SPACE WITH IMAGES OR WORDS
THAT COME TO MIND.

The best things that
happened today:

Things I wish I could
change about today:

I am proud of myself
today because...

I think I still need
to work on...

MY NIGHTLY REFLECTION PROMPTS

READ THE PROMPTS BELOW AND RESPOND BY FILLING IN
EACH SPACE WITH IMAGES OR WORDS THAT COME TO
MIND. LASTLY, REPEAT THE AFFIRMATION AT THE
BOTTOM OF THE PAGE OUT LOUD 3 TIMES.

My overall mood today:

calm   confident   nervous

happy   angry   grateful

sad   jealous   curious

Any others that came up:

My overall rating of the day:

1   2   3   4   5   6   7   8   9   10

Any and all other thoughts:

I RELEASE THIS DAY AND CALL BACK MY PEACE, POWER, AND POSITIVE ENERGY!

MY NIGHTLY REFLECTION PROMPTS

READ THE PROMPTS BELOW AND RESPOND BY
FILLING IN EACH SPACE WITH IMAGES OR WORDS
THAT COME TO MIND.

The best things that
happened today:

Things I wish I could
change about today:

I am proud of myself
today because...

I think I still need
to work on...

MY NIGHTLY REFLECTION PROMPTS

READ THE PROMPTS BELOW AND RESPOND BY FILLING IN
EACH SPACE WITH IMAGES OR WORDS THAT COME TO
MIND. LASTLY, REPEAT THE AFFIRMATION AT THE
BOTTOM OF THE PAGE OUT LOUD 3 TIMES.

My overall mood today:

calm	confident	nervous
happy	angry	grateful
sad	jealous	curious

Any others that came up:

My overall rating of the day:

1   2   3   4   5   6   7   8   9   10

Any and all other thoughts:

I RELEASE THIS DAY AND CALL BACK MY PEACE, POWER, AND POSITIVE ENERGY!

MY NIGHTLY REFLECTION PROMPTS

READ THE PROMPTS BELOW AND RESPOND BY
FILLING IN EACH SPACE WITH IMAGES OR WORDS
THAT COME TO MIND.

The best things that
happened today:

Things I wish I could
change about today:

I am proud of myself
today because...

I think I still need
to work on...

MY NIGHTLY
REFLECTION PROMPTS

READ THE PROMPTS BELOW AND RESPOND BY FILLING IN
EACH SPACE WITH IMAGES OR WORDS THAT COME TO
MIND. LASTLY, REPEAT THE AFFIRMATION AT THE
BOTTOM OF THE PAGE OUT LOUD 3 TIMES.

My overall mood today:

calm	confident	nervous
happy	angry	grateful
sad	jealous	curious

Any others that came up:

My overall rating of the day:

1   2   3   4   5   6   7   8   9   10

Any and all other thoughts:

I RELEASE THIS DAY AND CALL BACK MY PEACE, POWER, AND POSITIVE ENERGY!

MY NIGHTLY REFLECTION PROMPTS

READ THE PROMPTS BELOW AND RESPOND BY
FILLING IN EACH SPACE WITH IMAGES OR WORDS
THAT COME TO MIND.

The best things that
happened today:

Things I wish I could
change about today:

I am proud of myself
today because...

I think I still need
to work on...

MY NIGHTLY
REFLECTION PROMPTS

READ THE PROMPTS BELOW AND RESPOND BY FILLING IN
EACH SPACE WITH IMAGES OR WORDS THAT COME TO
MIND. LASTLY, REPEAT THE AFFIRMATION AT THE
BOTTOM OF THE PAGE OUT LOUD 3 TIMES.

My overall mood today:

calm   confident   nervous

happy   angry   grateful

sad   jealous   curious

Any others that came up:

My overall rating of the day:

1   2   3   4   5   6   7   8   9   10

Any and all other thoughts:

I RELEASE THIS DAY AND CALL BACK MY PEACE, POWER, AND POSITIVE ENERGY!

MY NIGHTLY
REFLECTION PROMPTS

READ THE PROMPTS BELOW AND RESPOND BY
FILLING IN EACH SPACE WITH IMAGES OR WORDS
THAT COME TO MIND.

The best things that
happened today:

Things I wish I could
change about today:

I am proud of myself
today because...

I think I still need
to work on...

MY NIGHTLY
REFLECTION PROMPTS

READ THE PROMPTS BELOW AND RESPOND BY FILLING IN
EACH SPACE WITH IMAGES OR WORDS THAT COME TO
MIND. LASTLY, REPEAT THE AFFIRMATION AT THE
BOTTOM OF THE PAGE OUT LOUD 3 TIMES.

My overall mood today:

calm   confident   nervous

happy   angry   grateful

sad   jealous   curious

Any others that came up:

My overall rating of the day:

1   2   3   4   5   6   7   8   9   10

Any and all other thoughts:

I RELEASE THIS DAY AND CALL BACK MY PEACE, POWER, AND POSITIVE ENERGY!

MY NIGHTLY
REFLECTION PROMPTS

READ THE PROMPTS BELOW AND RESPOND BY
FILLING IN EACH SPACE WITH IMAGES OR WORDS
THAT COME TO MIND.

The best things that
happened today:

Things I wish I could
change about today:

I am proud of myself
today because...

I think I still need
to work on...

MY NIGHTLY
REFLECTION PROMPTS

READ THE PROMPTS BELOW AND RESPOND BY FILLING IN
EACH SPACE WITH IMAGES OR WORDS THAT COME TO
MIND. LASTLY, REPEAT THE AFFIRMATION AT THE
BOTTOM OF THE PAGE OUT LOUD 3 TIMES.

My overall mood today:

calm	confident	nervous
happy	angry	grateful
sad	jealous	curious

Any others that came up:

My overall rating of the day:

1   2   3   4   5   6   7   8   9   10

Any and all other thoughts:

I RELEASE THIS DAY AND CALL BACK MY PEACE, POWER, AND POSITIVE ENERGY!

MY NIGHTLY REFLECTION PROMPTS

READ THE PROMPTS BELOW AND RESPOND BY
FILLING IN EACH SPACE WITH IMAGES OR WORDS
THAT COME TO MIND.

The best things that
happened today:

Things I wish I could
change about today:

I am proud of myself
today because...

I think I still need
to work on...

MY NIGHTLY REFLECTION PROMPTS

READ THE PROMPTS BELOW AND RESPOND BY FILLING IN
EACH SPACE WITH IMAGES OR WORDS THAT COME TO
MIND. LASTLY, REPEAT THE AFFIRMATION AT THE
BOTTOM OF THE PAGE OUT LOUD 3 TIMES.

My overall mood today:

calm   confident   nervous

happy   angry   grateful

sad   jealous   curious

Any others that came up:

My overall rating of the day:

1   2   3   4   5   6   7   8   9   10

Any and all other thoughts:

I RELEASE THIS DAY AND CALL BACK MY PEACE, POWER, AND POSITIVE ENERGY!

MY NIGHTLY
REFLECTION PROMPTS

READ THE PROMPTS BELOW AND RESPOND BY
FILLING IN EACH SPACE WITH IMAGES OR WORDS
THAT COME TO MIND.

The best things that
happened today:

Things I wish I could
change about today:

I am proud of myself
today because...

I think I still need
to work on...

MY NIGHTLY
REFLECTION PROMPTS

READ THE PROMPTS BELOW AND RESPOND BY FILLING IN
EACH SPACE WITH IMAGES OR WORDS THAT COME TO
MIND. LASTLY, REPEAT THE AFFIRMATION AT THE
BOTTOM OF THE PAGE OUT LOUD 3 TIMES.

My overall mood today:

calm   confident   nervous

happy   angry   grateful

sad   jealous   curious

Any others that came up:

My overall rating of the day:

1   2   3   4   5   6   7   8   9   10

Any and all other thoughts:

I RELEASE THIS DAY AND CALL BACK MY PEACE, POWER, AND POSITIVE ENERGY!

MY NIGHTLY
REFLECTION PROMPTS

READ THE PROMPTS BELOW AND RESPOND BY
FILLING IN EACH SPACE WITH IMAGES OR WORDS
THAT COME TO MIND.

The best things that
happened today:

Things I wish I could
change about today:

I am proud of myself
today because...

I think I still need
to work on...

MY NIGHTLY
REFLECTION PROMPTS

READ THE PROMPTS BELOW AND RESPOND BY FILLING IN
EACH SPACE WITH IMAGES OR WORDS THAT COME TO
MIND. LASTLY, REPEAT THE AFFIRMATION AT THE
BOTTOM OF THE PAGE OUT LOUD 3 TIMES.

My overall mood today:

calm	confident	nervous
happy	angry	grateful
sad	jealous	curious

Any others that came up:

My overall rating of the day:

1   2   3   4   5   6   7   8   9   10

Any and all other thoughts:

I RELEASE THIS DAY AND CALL BACK MY PEACE, POWER, AND POSITIVE ENERGY!

MY NIGHTLY
REFLECTION PROMPTS

READ THE PROMPTS BELOW AND RESPOND BY
FILLING IN EACH SPACE WITH IMAGES OR WORDS
THAT COME TO MIND.

The best things that
happened today:

Things I wish I could
change about today:

I am proud of myself
today because...

I think I still need
to work on...

MY NIGHTLY
REFLECTION PROMPTS

READ THE PROMPTS BELOW AND RESPOND BY FILLING IN
EACH SPACE WITH IMAGES OR WORDS THAT COME TO
MIND. LASTLY, REPEAT THE AFFIRMATION AT THE
BOTTOM OF THE PAGE OUT LOUD 3 TIMES.

My overall mood today:

calm   confident   nervous

happy   angry   grateful

sad   jealous   curious

Any others that came up:

My overall rating of the day:

1   2   3   4   5   6   7   8   9   10

Any and all other thoughts:

I RELEASE THIS DAY AND CALL BACK MY PEACE, POWER, AND POSITIVE ENERGY!

MY NIGHTLY
REFLECTION PROMPTS

READ THE PROMPTS BELOW AND RESPOND BY
FILLING IN EACH SPACE WITH IMAGES OR WORDS
THAT COME TO MIND.

The best things that
happened today:

Things I wish I could
change about today:

I am proud of myself
today because...

I think I still need
to work on...

MY NIGHTLY
REFLECTION PROMPTS

READ THE PROMPTS BELOW AND RESPOND BY FILLING IN
EACH SPACE WITH IMAGES OR WORDS THAT COME TO
MIND. LASTLY, REPEAT THE AFFIRMATION AT THE
BOTTOM OF THE PAGE OUT LOUD 3 TIMES.

My overall mood today:

calm	confident	nervous
happy	angry	grateful
sad	jealous	curious

Any others that came up:

My overall rating of the day:

1   2   3   4   5   6   7   8   9   10

Any and all other thoughts:

I RELEASE THIS DAY AND CALL BACK MY PEACE, POWER, AND POSITIVE ENERGY!

MY NIGHTLY
REFLECTION PROMPTS

READ THE PROMPTS BELOW AND RESPOND BY
FILLING IN EACH SPACE WITH IMAGES OR WORDS
THAT COME TO MIND.

The best things that
happened today:

Things I wish I could
change about today:

I am proud of myself
today because...

I think I still need
to work on...

MY NIGHTLY
REFLECTION PROMPTS

READ THE PROMPTS BELOW AND RESPOND BY FILLING IN
EACH SPACE WITH IMAGES OR WORDS THAT COME TO
MIND. LASTLY, REPEAT THE AFFIRMATION AT THE
BOTTOM OF THE PAGE OUT LOUD 3 TIMES.

My overall mood today:

calm   confident   nervous

happy   angry   grateful

sad   jealous   curious

Any others that came up:

My overall rating of the day:

1   2   3   4   5   6   7   8   9   10

Any and all other thoughts:

I RELEASE THIS DAY AND CALL BACK MY PEACE, POWER, AND POSITIVE ENERGY!

MY NIGHTLY
REFLECTION PROMPTS

READ THE PROMPTS BELOW AND RESPOND BY
FILLING IN EACH SPACE WITH IMAGES OR WORDS
THAT COME TO MIND.

The best things that
happened today:

Things I wish I could
change about today:

I am proud of myself
today because...

I think I still need
to work on...

MY NIGHTLY
REFLECTION PROMPTS

READ THE PROMPTS BELOW AND RESPOND BY FILLING IN
EACH SPACE WITH IMAGES OR WORDS THAT COME TO
MIND. LASTLY, REPEAT THE AFFIRMATION AT THE
BOTTOM OF THE PAGE OUT LOUD 3 TIMES.

My overall mood today:

calm	confident	nervous
happy	angry	grateful
sad	jealous	curious

Any others that came up:

My overall rating of the day:

1 2 3 4 5 6 7 8 9 10

Any and all other thoughts:

I RELEASE THIS DAY AND CALL BACK MY PEACE, POWER, AND POSITIVE ENERGY!

MY NIGHTLY
REFLECTION PROMPTS

READ THE PROMPTS BELOW AND RESPOND BY
FILLING IN EACH SPACE WITH IMAGES OR WORDS
THAT COME TO MIND.

The best things that
happened today:

Things I wish I could
change about today:

I am proud of myself
today because...

I think I still need
to work on...

MY NIGHTLY REFLECTION PROMPTS

READ THE PROMPTS BELOW AND RESPOND BY FILLING IN
EACH SPACE WITH IMAGES OR WORDS THAT COME TO
MIND. LASTLY, REPEAT THE AFFIRMATION AT THE
BOTTOM OF THE PAGE OUT LOUD 3 TIMES.

My overall mood today:

calm   confident   nervous

happy   angry   grateful

sad   jealous   curious

Any others that came up:

My overall rating of the day:

1   2   3   4   5   6   7   8   9   10

Any and all other thoughts:

I RELEASE THIS DAY AND CALL BACK MY PEACE, POWER, AND POSITIVE ENERGY!

MY NIGHTLY REFLECTION PROMPTS

READ THE PROMPTS BELOW AND RESPOND BY
FILLING IN EACH SPACE WITH IMAGES OR WORDS
THAT COME TO MIND.

The best things that
happened today:

Things I wish I could
change about today:

I am proud of myself
today because...

I think I still need
to work on...

MY NIGHTLY REFLECTION PROMPTS

READ THE PROMPTS BELOW AND RESPOND BY FILLING IN
EACH SPACE WITH IMAGES OR WORDS THAT COME TO
MIND. LASTLY, REPEAT THE AFFIRMATION AT THE
BOTTOM OF THE PAGE OUT LOUD 3 TIMES.

My overall mood today:

calm   confident   nervous

happy   angry   grateful

sad   jealous   curious

Any others that came up:

My overall rating of the day:

1   2   3   4   5   6   7   8   9   10

Any and all other thoughts:

I RELEASE THIS DAY AND CALL BACK MY PEACE, POWER, AND POSITIVE ENERGY!

MY NIGHTLY
REFLECTION PROMPTS

READ THE PROMPTS BELOW AND RESPOND BY
FILLING IN EACH SPACE WITH IMAGES OR WORDS
THAT COME TO MIND.

The best things that
happened today:

Things I wish I could
change about today:

I am proud of myself
today because...

I think I still need
to work on...

MY NIGHTLY
REFLECTION PROMPTS

READ THE PROMPTS BELOW AND RESPOND BY FILLING IN
EACH SPACE WITH IMAGES OR WORDS THAT COME TO
MIND. LASTLY, REPEAT THE AFFIRMATION AT THE
BOTTOM OF THE PAGE OUT LOUD 3 TIMES.

My overall mood today:

calm	confident	nervous
happy	angry	grateful
sad	jealous	curious

Any others that came up:

My overall rating of the day:

1   2   3   4   5   6   7   8   9   10

Any and all other thoughts:

I RELEASE THIS DAY AND CALL BACK MY PEACE, POWER, AND POSITIVE ENERGY!

MY NIGHTLY
REFLECTION PROMPTS

READ THE PROMPTS BELOW AND RESPOND BY
FILLING IN EACH SPACE WITH IMAGES OR WORDS
THAT COME TO MIND.

The best things that
happened today:

Things I wish I could
change about today:

I am proud of myself
today because...

I think I still need
to work on...

MY NIGHTLY
REFLECTION PROMPTS

READ THE PROMPTS BELOW AND RESPOND BY FILLING IN
EACH SPACE WITH IMAGES OR WORDS THAT COME TO
MIND. LASTLY, REPEAT THE AFFIRMATION AT THE
BOTTOM OF THE PAGE OUT LOUD 3 TIMES.

My overall mood today:

calm   confident   nervous

happy   angry   grateful

sad   jealous   curious

Any others that came up:

My overall rating of the day:

1   2   3   4   5   6   7   8   9   10

Any and all other thoughts:

I RELEASE THIS DAY AND CALL BACK MY PEACE, POWER, AND POSITIVE ENERGY!

MY NIGHTLY
REFLECTION PROMPTS

READ THE PROMPTS BELOW AND RESPOND BY
FILLING IN EACH SPACE WITH IMAGES OR WORDS
THAT COME TO MIND.

The best things that
happened today:

Things I wish I could
change about today:

I am proud of myself
today because...

I think I still need
to work on...

MY NIGHTLY REFLECTION PROMPTS

READ THE PROMPTS BELOW AND RESPOND BY FILLING IN
EACH SPACE WITH IMAGES OR WORDS THAT COME TO
MIND. LASTLY, REPEAT THE AFFIRMATION AT THE
BOTTOM OF THE PAGE OUT LOUD 3 TIMES.

My overall mood today:

calm   confident   nervous

happy   angry   grateful

sad   jealous   curious

Any others that came up:

My overall rating of the day:

1   2   3   4   5   6   7   8   9   10

Any and all other thoughts:

I RELEASE THIS DAY AND CALL BACK MY PEACE, POWER, AND POSITIVE ENERGY!

MY NIGHTLY
REFLECTION PROMPTS

READ THE PROMPTS BELOW AND RESPOND BY
FILLING IN EACH SPACE WITH IMAGES OR WORDS
THAT COME TO MIND.

The best things that
happened today:

Things I wish I could
change about today:

I am proud of myself
today because...

I think I still need
to work on...

MY NIGHTLY REFLECTION PROMPTS

READ THE PROMPTS BELOW AND RESPOND BY FILLING IN
EACH SPACE WITH IMAGES OR WORDS THAT COME TO
MIND. LASTLY, REPEAT THE AFFIRMATION AT THE
BOTTOM OF THE PAGE OUT LOUD 3 TIMES.

My overall mood today:

calm	confident	nervous
happy	angry	grateful
sad	jealous	curious

Any others that came up:

My overall rating of the day:

1   2   3   4   5   6   7   8   9   10

Any and all other thoughts:

I RELEASE THIS DAY AND CALL BACK MY PEACE, POWER, AND POSITIVE ENERGY!

MY NIGHTLY
REFLECTION PROMPTS

READ THE PROMPTS BELOW AND RESPOND BY
FILLING IN EACH SPACE WITH IMAGES OR WORDS
THAT COME TO MIND.

The best things that
happened today:

Things I wish I could
change about today:

I am proud of myself
today because...

I think I still need
to work on...

MY NIGHTLY
REFLECTION PROMPTS

READ THE PROMPTS BELOW AND RESPOND BY FILLING IN
EACH SPACE WITH IMAGES OR WORDS THAT COME TO
MIND. LASTLY, REPEAT THE AFFIRMATION AT THE
BOTTOM OF THE PAGE OUT LOUD 3 TIMES.

My overall mood today:

calm	confident	nervous
happy	angry	grateful
sad	jealous	curious

Any others that came up:

My overall rating of the day:

1   2   3   4   5   6   7   8   9   10

Any and all other thoughts:

I RELEASE THIS DAY AND CALL BACK MY PEACE, POWER, AND POSITIVE ENERGY!

MY NIGHTLY
REFLECTION PROMPTS

READ THE PROMPTS BELOW AND RESPOND BY
FILLING IN EACH SPACE WITH IMAGES OR WORDS
THAT COME TO MIND.

The best things that
happened today:

Things I wish I could
change about today:

I am proud of myself
today because...

I think I still need
to work on...

MY NIGHTLY
REFLECTION PROMPTS

READ THE PROMPTS BELOW AND RESPOND BY FILLING IN
EACH SPACE WITH IMAGES OR WORDS THAT COME TO
MIND. LASTLY, REPEAT THE AFFIRMATION AT THE
BOTTOM OF THE PAGE OUT LOUD 3 TIMES.

My overall mood today:

calm   confident   nervous

happy   angry   grateful

sad   jealous   curious

Any others that came up:

My overall rating of the day:

1   2   3   4   5   6   7   8   9   10

Any and all other thoughts:

I RELEASE THIS DAY AND CALL BACK MY PEACE, POWER, AND POSITIVE ENERGY!

MY NIGHTLY REFLECTION PROMPTS

READ THE PROMPTS BELOW AND RESPOND BY
FILLING IN EACH SPACE WITH IMAGES OR WORDS
THAT COME TO MIND.

The best things that
happened today:

Things I wish I could
change about today:

I am proud of myself
today because...

I think I still need
to work on...

MY NIGHTLY
REFLECTION PROMPTS

READ THE PROMPTS BELOW AND RESPOND BY FILLING IN
EACH SPACE WITH IMAGES OR WORDS THAT COME TO
MIND. LASTLY, REPEAT THE AFFIRMATION AT THE
BOTTOM OF THE PAGE OUT LOUD 3 TIMES.

My overall mood today:

calm	confident	nervous
happy	angry	grateful
sad	jealous	curious

Any others that came up:

My overall rating of the day:

1   2   3   4   5   6   7   8   9   10

Any and all other thoughts:

I RELEASE THIS DAY AND CALL BACK MY PEACE, POWER, AND POSITIVE ENERGY!

MY NIGHTLY
REFLECTION PROMPTS

READ THE PROMPTS BELOW AND RESPOND BY
FILLING IN EACH SPACE WITH IMAGES OR WORDS
THAT COME TO MIND.

The best things that
happened today:

Things I wish I could
change about today:

I am proud of myself
today because...

I think I still need
to work on...

MY NIGHTLY
REFLECTION PROMPTS

READ THE PROMPTS BELOW AND RESPOND BY FILLING IN
EACH SPACE WITH IMAGES OR WORDS THAT COME TO
MIND. LASTLY, REPEAT THE AFFIRMATION AT THE
BOTTOM OF THE PAGE OUT LOUD 3 TIMES.

My overall mood today:

calm	confident	nervous
happy	angry	grateful
sad	jealous	curious

Any others that came up:

My overall rating of the day:

1   2   3   4   5   6   7   8   9   10

Any and all other thoughts:

I RELEASE THIS DAY AND CALL BACK MY PEACE, POWER, AND POSITIVE ENERGY!

MY NIGHTLY
REFLECTION PROMPTS

READ THE PROMPTS BELOW AND RESPOND BY
FILLING IN EACH SPACE WITH IMAGES OR WORDS
THAT COME TO MIND.

The best things that
happened today:

Things I wish I could
change about today:

I am proud of myself
today because...

I think I still need
to work on...

MY NIGHTLY
REFLECTION PROMPTS

READ THE PROMPTS BELOW AND RESPOND BY FILLING IN
EACH SPACE WITH IMAGES OR WORDS THAT COME TO
MIND. LASTLY, REPEAT THE AFFIRMATION AT THE
BOTTOM OF THE PAGE OUT LOUD 3 TIMES.

My overall mood today:

calm	confident	nervous
happy	angry	grateful
sad	jealous	curious

Any others that came up:

My overall rating of the day:

1   2   3   4   5   6   7   8   9   10

Any and all other thoughts:

I RELEASE THIS DAY AND CALL BACK MY PEACE, POWER, AND POSITIVE ENERGY!

MY NIGHTLY
REFLECTION PROMPTS

READ THE PROMPTS BELOW AND RESPOND BY
FILLING IN EACH SPACE WITH IMAGES OR WORDS
THAT COME TO MIND.

The best things that
happened today:

Things I wish I could
change about today:

I am proud of myself
today because...

I think I still need
to work on...

MY NIGHTLY REFLECTION PROMPTS

READ THE PROMPTS BELOW AND RESPOND BY FILLING IN
EACH SPACE WITH IMAGES OR WORDS THAT COME TO
MIND. LASTLY, REPEAT THE AFFIRMATION AT THE
BOTTOM OF THE PAGE OUT LOUD 3 TIMES.

My overall mood today:

calm	confident	nervous
happy	angry	grateful
sad	jealous	curious

Any others that came up:

My overall rating of the day:

1   2   3   4   5   6   7   8   9   10

Any and all other thoughts:

I RELEASE THIS DAY AND CALL BACK MY PEACE, POWER, AND POSITIVE ENERGY!

MY NIGHTLY
REFLECTION PROMPTS

READ THE PROMPTS BELOW AND RESPOND BY
FILLING IN EACH SPACE WITH IMAGES OR WORDS
THAT COME TO MIND.

The best things that
happened today:

Things I wish I could
change about today:

I am proud of myself
today because...

I think I still need
to work on...

MY NIGHTLY
REFLECTION PROMPTS

READ THE PROMPTS BELOW AND RESPOND BY FILLING IN
EACH SPACE WITH IMAGES OR WORDS THAT COME TO
MIND. LASTLY, REPEAT THE AFFIRMATION AT THE
BOTTOM OF THE PAGE OUT LOUD 3 TIMES.

My overall mood today:

calm	confident	nervous
happy	angry	grateful
sad	jealous	curious

Any others that came up:

My overall rating of the day:

1   2   3   4   5   6   7   8   9   10

Any and all other thoughts:

I RELEASE THIS DAY AND CALL BACK MY PEACE, POWER, AND POSITIVE ENERGY!

MY NIGHTLY REFLECTION PROMPTS

READ THE PROMPTS BELOW AND RESPOND BY
FILLING IN EACH SPACE WITH IMAGES OR WORDS
THAT COME TO MIND.

The best things that
happened today:

Things I wish I could
change about today:

I am proud of myself
today because...

I think I still need
to work on...

MY NIGHTLY
REFLECTION PROMPTS

READ THE PROMPTS BELOW AND RESPOND BY FILLING IN
EACH SPACE WITH IMAGES OR WORDS THAT COME TO
MIND. LASTLY, REPEAT THE AFFIRMATION AT THE
BOTTOM OF THE PAGE OUT LOUD 3 TIMES.

My overall mood today:

calm	confident	nervous
happy	angry	grateful
sad	jealous	curious

Any others that came up:

My overall rating of the day:

1   2   3   4   5   6   7   8   9   10

Any and all other thoughts:

I RELEASE THIS DAY AND CALL BACK MY PEACE, POWER, AND POSITIVE ENERGY!

MY NIGHTLY
REFLECTION PROMPTS

READ THE PROMPTS BELOW AND RESPOND BY
FILLING IN EACH SPACE WITH IMAGES OR WORDS
THAT COME TO MIND.

The best things that
happened today:

Things I wish I could
change about today:

I am proud of myself
today because...

I think I still need
to work on...

MY NIGHTLY REFLECTION PROMPTS

READ THE PROMPTS BELOW AND RESPOND BY FILLING IN
EACH SPACE WITH IMAGES OR WORDS THAT COME TO
MIND. LASTLY, REPEAT THE AFFIRMATION AT THE
BOTTOM OF THE PAGE OUT LOUD 3 TIMES.

My overall mood today:

calm   confident   nervous

happy   angry   grateful

sad   jealous   curious

Any others that came up:

My overall rating of the day:

1   2   3   4   5   6   7   8   9   10

Any and all other thoughts:

I RELEASE THIS DAY AND CALL BACK MY PEACE, POWER, AND POSITIVE ENERGY!

MY NIGHTLY
REFLECTION PROMPTS

READ THE PROMPTS BELOW AND RESPOND BY
FILLING IN EACH SPACE WITH IMAGES OR WORDS
THAT COME TO MIND.

The best things that
happened today:

Things I wish I could
change about today:

I am proud of myself
today because...

I think I still need
to work on...

MY NIGHTLY REFLECTION PROMPTS

READ THE PROMPTS BELOW AND RESPOND BY FILLING IN
EACH SPACE WITH IMAGES OR WORDS THAT COME TO
MIND. LASTLY, REPEAT THE AFFIRMATION AT THE
BOTTOM OF THE PAGE OUT LOUD 3 TIMES.

My overall mood today:

calm	confident	nervous
happy	angry	grateful
sad	jealous	curious

Any others that came up:

My overall rating of the day:

1   2   3   4   5   6   7   8   9   10

Any and all other thoughts:

I RELEASE THIS DAY AND CALL BACK MY PEACE, POWER, AND POSITIVE ENERGY!

MY NIGHTLY
REFLECTION PROMPTS

READ THE PROMPTS BELOW AND RESPOND BY
FILLING IN EACH SPACE WITH IMAGES OR WORDS
THAT COME TO MIND.

The best things that
happened today:

Things I wish I could
change about today:

I am proud of myself
today because...

I think I still need
to work on...

MY NIGHTLY REFLECTION PROMPTS

READ THE PROMPTS BELOW AND RESPOND BY FILLING IN
EACH SPACE WITH IMAGES OR WORDS THAT COME TO
MIND. LASTLY, REPEAT THE AFFIRMATION AT THE
BOTTOM OF THE PAGE OUT LOUD 3 TIMES.

My overall mood today:

calm	confident	nervous
happy	angry	grateful
sad	jealous	curious

Any others that came up:

My overall rating of the day:

1   2   3   4   5   6   7   8   9   10

Any and all other thoughts:

I RELEASE THIS DAY AND CALL BACK MY PEACE, POWER, AND POSITIVE ENERGY!

MY NIGHTLY
REFLECTION PROMPTS

READ THE PROMPTS BELOW AND RESPOND BY
FILLING IN EACH SPACE WITH IMAGES OR WORDS
THAT COME TO MIND.

The best things that
happened today:

Things I wish I could
change about today:

I am proud of myself
today because...

I think I still need
to work on...

MY NIGHTLY
REFLECTION PROMPTS

READ THE PROMPTS BELOW AND RESPOND BY FILLING IN
EACH SPACE WITH IMAGES OR WORDS THAT COME TO
MIND. LASTLY, REPEAT THE AFFIRMATION AT THE
BOTTOM OF THE PAGE OUT LOUD 3 TIMES.

My overall mood today:

calm   confident   nervous

happy   angry   grateful

sad   jealous   curious

Any others that came up:

My overall rating of the day:

1   2   3   4   5   6   7   8   9   10

Any and all other thoughts:

I RELEASE THIS DAY AND CALL BACK MY PEACE, POWER, AND POSITIVE ENERGY!

MY NIGHTLY
REFLECTION PROMPTS

READ THE PROMPTS BELOW AND RESPOND BY
FILLING IN EACH SPACE WITH IMAGES OR WORDS
THAT COME TO MIND.

The best things that
happened today:

Things I wish I could
change about today:

I am proud of myself
today because...

I think I still need
to work on...

MY NIGHTLY
REFLECTION PROMPTS

READ THE PROMPTS BELOW AND RESPOND BY FILLING IN
EACH SPACE WITH IMAGES OR WORDS THAT COME TO
MIND. LASTLY, REPEAT THE AFFIRMATION AT THE
BOTTOM OF THE PAGE OUT LOUD 3 TIMES.

My overall mood today:

calm	confident	nervous
happy	angry	grateful
sad	jealous	curious

Any others that came up:

My overall rating of the day:

1   2   3   4   5   6   7   8   9   10

Any and all other thoughts:

I RELEASE THIS DAY AND CALL BACK MY PEACE, POWER, AND POSITIVE ENERGY!

MY NIGHTLY
REFLECTION PROMPTS

READ THE PROMPTS BELOW AND RESPOND BY
FILLING IN EACH SPACE WITH IMAGES OR WORDS
THAT COME TO MIND.

The best things that
happened today:

Things I wish I could
change about today:

I am proud of myself
today because...

I think I still need
to work on...

MY NIGHTLY REFLECTION PROMPTS

READ THE PROMPTS BELOW AND RESPOND BY FILLING IN
EACH SPACE WITH IMAGES OR WORDS THAT COME TO
MIND. LASTLY, REPEAT THE AFFIRMATION AT THE
BOTTOM OF THE PAGE OUT LOUD 3 TIMES.

My overall mood today:

calm	confident	nervous
happy	angry	grateful
sad	jealous	curious

Any others that came up:

My overall rating of the day:

1   2   3   4   5   6   7   8   9   10

Any and all other thoughts:

I RELEASE THIS DAY AND CALL BACK MY PEACE, POWER, AND POSITIVE ENERGY!

MY NIGHTLY
REFLECTION PROMPTS

READ THE PROMPTS BELOW AND RESPOND BY
FILLING IN EACH SPACE WITH IMAGES OR WORDS
THAT COME TO MIND.

The best things that
happened today:

Things I wish I could
change about today:

I am proud of myself
today because...

I think I still need
to work on...

MY NIGHTLY
REFLECTION PROMPTS

READ THE PROMPTS BELOW AND RESPOND BY FILLING IN
EACH SPACE WITH IMAGES OR WORDS THAT COME TO
MIND. LASTLY, REPEAT THE AFFIRMATION AT THE
BOTTOM OF THE PAGE OUT LOUD 3 TIMES.

My overall mood today:

calm	confident	nervous
happy	angry	grateful
sad	jealous	curious

Any others that came up:

My overall rating of the day:

1   2   3   4   5   6   7   8   9   10

Any and all other thoughts:

I RELEASE THIS DAY AND CALL BACK MY PEACE, POWER, AND POSITIVE ENERGY!

MY NIGHTLY REFLECTION PROMPTS

READ THE PROMPTS BELOW AND RESPOND BY
FILLING IN EACH SPACE WITH IMAGES OR WORDS
THAT COME TO MIND.

The best things that
happened today:

Things I wish I could
change about today:

I am proud of myself
today because...

I think I still need
to work on...

MY NIGHTLY
REFLECTION PROMPTS

READ THE PROMPTS BELOW AND RESPOND BY FILLING IN
EACH SPACE WITH IMAGES OR WORDS THAT COME TO
MIND. LASTLY, REPEAT THE AFFIRMATION AT THE
BOTTOM OF THE PAGE OUT LOUD 3 TIMES.

My overall mood today:

calm   confident   nervous

happy   angry   grateful

sad   jealous   curious

Any others that came up:

My overall rating of the day:

1   2   3   4   5   6   7   8   9   10

Any and all other thoughts:

I RELEASE THIS DAY AND CALL BACK MY PEACE, POWER, AND POSITIVE ENERGY!

MY NIGHTLY
REFLECTION PROMPTS

READ THE PROMPTS BELOW AND RESPOND BY
FILLING IN EACH SPACE WITH IMAGES OR WORDS
THAT COME TO MIND.

The best things that
happened today:

Things I wish I could
change about today:

I am proud of myself
today because...

I think I still need
to work on...

MY NIGHTLY
REFLECTION PROMPTS

READ THE PROMPTS BELOW AND RESPOND BY FILLING IN
EACH SPACE WITH IMAGES OR WORDS THAT COME TO
MIND. LASTLY, REPEAT THE AFFIRMATION AT THE
BOTTOM OF THE PAGE OUT LOUD 3 TIMES.

My overall mood today:

calm	confident	nervous
happy	angry	grateful
sad	jealous	curious

Any others that came up:

My overall rating of the day:

1   2   3   4   5   6   7   8   9   10

Any and all other thoughts:

I RELEASE THIS DAY AND CALL BACK MY PEACE, POWER, AND POSITIVE ENERGY!

MY NIGHTLY
REFLECTION PROMPTS

READ THE PROMPTS BELOW AND RESPOND BY
FILLING IN EACH SPACE WITH IMAGES OR WORDS
THAT COME TO MIND.

The best things that
happened today:

Things I wish I could
change about today:

I am proud of myself
today because...

I think I still need
to work on...

MY NIGHTLY REFLECTION PROMPTS

READ THE PROMPTS BELOW AND RESPOND BY FILLING IN
EACH SPACE WITH IMAGES OR WORDS THAT COME TO
MIND. LASTLY, REPEAT THE AFFIRMATION AT THE
BOTTOM OF THE PAGE OUT LOUD 3 TIMES.

My overall mood today:

calm   confident   nervous

happy   angry   grateful

sad   jealous   curious

Any others that came up:

My overall rating of the day:

1   2   3   4   5   6   7   8   9   10

Any and all other thoughts:

I RELEASE THIS DAY AND CALL BACK MY PEACE, POWER, AND POSITIVE ENERGY!

MY NIGHTLY
REFLECTION PROMPTS

READ THE PROMPTS BELOW AND RESPOND BY
FILLING IN EACH SPACE WITH IMAGES OR WORDS
THAT COME TO MIND.

The best things that
happened today:

Things I wish I could
change about today:

I am proud of myself
today because...

I think I still need
to work on...

MY NIGHTLY
REFLECTION PROMPTS

READ THE PROMPTS BELOW AND RESPOND BY FILLING IN
EACH SPACE WITH IMAGES OR WORDS THAT COME TO
MIND. LASTLY, REPEAT THE AFFIRMATION AT THE
BOTTOM OF THE PAGE OUT LOUD 3 TIMES.

My overall mood today:

calm   confident   nervous

happy   angry   grateful

sad   jealous   curious

Any others that came up:

My overall rating of the day:

1   2   3   4   5   6   7   8   9   10

Any and all other thoughts:

I RELEASE THIS DAY AND CALL BACK MY PEACE, POWER, AND POSITIVE ENERGY!

MY NIGHTLY
REFLECTION PROMPTS

READ THE PROMPTS BELOW AND RESPOND BY
FILLING IN EACH SPACE WITH IMAGES OR WORDS
THAT COME TO MIND.

The best things that
happened today:

Things I wish I could
change about today:

I am proud of myself
today because...

I think I still need
to work on...

MY NIGHTLY
REFLECTION PROMPTS

READ THE PROMPTS BELOW AND RESPOND BY FILLING IN
EACH SPACE WITH IMAGES OR WORDS THAT COME TO
MIND. LASTLY, REPEAT THE AFFIRMATION AT THE
BOTTOM OF THE PAGE OUT LOUD 3 TIMES.

My overall mood today:

calm	confident	nervous
happy	angry	grateful
sad	jealous	curious

Any others that came up:

My overall rating of the day:

1   2   3   4   5   6   7   8   9   10

Any and all other thoughts:

I RELEASE THIS DAY AND CALL BACK MY PEACE, POWER, AND POSITIVE ENERGY!

MY NIGHTLY REFLECTION PROMPTS

READ THE PROMPTS BELOW AND RESPOND BY
FILLING IN EACH SPACE WITH IMAGES OR WORDS
THAT COME TO MIND.

The best things that
happened today:

Things I wish I could
change about today:

I am proud of myself
today because...

I think I still need
to work on...

MY NIGHTLY REFLECTION PROMPTS

READ THE PROMPTS BELOW AND RESPOND BY FILLING IN EACH SPACE WITH IMAGES OR WORDS THAT COME TO MIND. LASTLY, REPEAT THE AFFIRMATION AT THE BOTTOM OF THE PAGE OUT LOUD 3 TIMES.

My overall mood today:

calm   confident   nervous

happy   angry   grateful

sad   jealous   curious

Any others that came up:

My overall rating of the day:

1   2   3   4   5   6   7   8   9   10

Any and all other thoughts:

I RELEASE THIS DAY AND CALL BACK MY PEACE, POWER, AND POSITIVE ENERGY!

MY NIGHTLY
REFLECTION PROMPTS

READ THE PROMPTS BELOW AND RESPOND BY
FILLING IN EACH SPACE WITH IMAGES OR WORDS
THAT COME TO MIND.

The best things that
happened today:

Things I wish I could
change about today:

I am proud of myself
today because...

I think I still need
to work on...

MY NIGHTLY
REFLECTION PROMPTS

READ THE PROMPTS BELOW AND RESPOND BY FILLING IN
EACH SPACE WITH IMAGES OR WORDS THAT COME TO
MIND. LASTLY, REPEAT THE AFFIRMATION AT THE
BOTTOM OF THE PAGE OUT LOUD 3 TIMES.

My overall mood today:

calm	confident	nervous
happy	angry	grateful
sad	jealous	curious

Any others that came up:

My overall rating of the day:

1   2   3   4   5   6   7   8   9   10

Any and all other thoughts:

I RELEASE THIS DAY AND CALL BACK MY PEACE, POWER, AND POSITIVE ENERGY!

MY NIGHTLY REFLECTION PROMPTS

READ THE PROMPTS BELOW AND RESPOND BY
FILLING IN EACH SPACE WITH IMAGES OR WORDS
THAT COME TO MIND.

The best things that
happened today:

Things I wish I could
change about today:

I am proud of myself
today because...

I think I still need
to work on...

MY NIGHTLY REFLECTION PROMPTS

READ THE PROMPTS BELOW AND RESPOND BY FILLING IN
EACH SPACE WITH IMAGES OR WORDS THAT COME TO
MIND. LASTLY, REPEAT THE AFFIRMATION AT THE
BOTTOM OF THE PAGE OUT LOUD 3 TIMES.

My overall mood today:

calm   confident   nervous

happy   angry   grateful

sad   jealous   curious

Any others that came up:

My overall rating of the day:

1   2   3   4   5   6   7   8   9   10

Any and all other thoughts:

I RELEASE THIS DAY AND CALL BACK MY PEACE, POWER, AND POSITIVE ENERGY!

MY NIGHTLY
REFLECTION PROMPTS

READ THE PROMPTS BELOW AND RESPOND BY
FILLING IN EACH SPACE WITH IMAGES OR WORDS
THAT COME TO MIND.

The best things that
happened today:

Things I wish I could
change about today:

I am proud of myself
today because...

I think I still need
to work on...

MY NIGHTLY
REFLECTION PROMPTS

READ THE PROMPTS BELOW AND RESPOND BY FILLING IN
EACH SPACE WITH IMAGES OR WORDS THAT COME TO
MIND. LASTLY, REPEAT THE AFFIRMATION AT THE
BOTTOM OF THE PAGE OUT LOUD 3 TIMES.

My overall mood today:

calm	confident	nervous
happy	angry	grateful
sad	jealous	curious

Any others that came up:

My overall rating of the day:

1   2   3   4   5   6   7   8   9   10

Any and all other thoughts:

I RELEASE THIS DAY AND CALL BACK MY PEACE, POWER, AND POSITIVE ENERGY!

MY NIGHTLY REFLECTION PROMPTS

READ THE PROMPTS BELOW AND RESPOND BY
FILLING IN EACH SPACE WITH IMAGES OR WORDS
THAT COME TO MIND.

The best things that
happened today:

Things I wish I could
change about today:

I am proud of myself
today because...

I think I still need
to work on...

MY NIGHTLY REFLECTION PROMPTS

READ THE PROMPTS BELOW AND RESPOND BY FILLING IN
EACH SPACE WITH IMAGES OR WORDS THAT COME TO
MIND. LASTLY, REPEAT THE AFFIRMATION AT THE
BOTTOM OF THE PAGE OUT LOUD 3 TIMES.

My overall mood today:

calm	confident	nervous
happy	angry	grateful
sad	jealous	curious

Any others that came up:

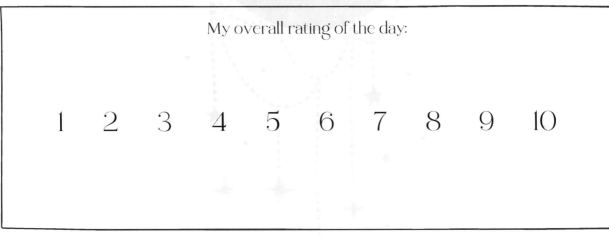

My overall rating of the day:

1   2   3   4   5   6   7   8   9   10

Any and all other thoughts:

I RELEASE THIS DAY AND CALL BACK MY PEACE, POWER, AND POSITIVE ENERGY!

MY NIGHTLY
REFLECTION PROMPTS

READ THE PROMPTS BELOW AND RESPOND BY
FILLING IN EACH SPACE WITH IMAGES OR WORDS
THAT COME TO MIND.

The best things that
happened today:

Things I wish I could
change about today:

I am proud of myself
today because...

I think I still need
to work on...

MY NIGHTLY
REFLECTION PROMPTS

READ THE PROMPTS BELOW AND RESPOND BY FILLING IN
EACH SPACE WITH IMAGES OR WORDS THAT COME TO
MIND. LASTLY, REPEAT THE AFFIRMATION AT THE
BOTTOM OF THE PAGE OUT LOUD 3 TIMES.

My overall mood today:

calm	confident	nervous
happy	angry	grateful
sad	jealous	curious

Any others that came up:

My overall rating of the day:

1   2   3   4   5   6   7   8   9   10

Any and all other thoughts:

I RELEASE THIS DAY AND CALL BACK MY PEACE, POWER, AND POSITIVE ENERGY!

MY NIGHTLY REFLECTION PROMPTS

READ THE PROMPTS BELOW AND RESPOND BY
FILLING IN EACH SPACE WITH IMAGES OR WORDS
THAT COME TO MIND.

The best things that
happened today:

Things I wish I could
change about today:

I am proud of myself
today because...

I think I still need
to work on...

MY NIGHTLY
REFLECTION PROMPTS

READ THE PROMPTS BELOW AND RESPOND BY FILLING IN
EACH SPACE WITH IMAGES OR WORDS THAT COME TO
MIND. LASTLY, REPEAT THE AFFIRMATION AT THE
BOTTOM OF THE PAGE OUT LOUD 3 TIMES.

My overall mood today:

calm	confident	nervous
happy	angry	grateful
sad	jealous	curious

Any others that came up:

My overall rating of the day:

1   2   3   4   5   6   7   8   9   10

Any and all other thoughts:

I RELEASE THIS DAY AND CALL BACK MY PEACE, POWER, AND POSITIVE ENERGY!

MY NIGHTLY
REFLECTION PROMPTS

READ THE PROMPTS BELOW AND RESPOND BY
FILLING IN EACH SPACE WITH IMAGES OR WORDS
THAT COME TO MIND.

The best things that
happened today:

Things I wish I could
change about today:

I am proud of myself
today because...

I think I still need
to work on...

MY NIGHTLY REFLECTION PROMPTS

READ THE PROMPTS BELOW AND RESPOND BY FILLING IN
EACH SPACE WITH IMAGES OR WORDS THAT COME TO
MIND. LASTLY, REPEAT THE AFFIRMATION AT THE
BOTTOM OF THE PAGE OUT LOUD 3 TIMES.

My overall mood today:

calm	confident	nervous
happy	angry	grateful
sad	jealous	curious

Any others that came up:

My overall rating of the day:

1   2   3   4   5   6   7   8   9   10

Any and all other thoughts:

I RELEASE THIS DAY AND CALL BACK MY PEACE, POWER, AND POSITIVE ENERGY!

MY NIGHTLY
REFLECTION PROMPTS

READ THE PROMPTS BELOW AND RESPOND BY
FILLING IN EACH SPACE WITH IMAGES OR WORDS
THAT COME TO MIND.

The best things that
happened today:

Things I wish I could
change about today:

I am proud of myself
today because...

I think I still need
to work on...

MY NIGHTLY REFLECTION PROMPTS

READ THE PROMPTS BELOW AND RESPOND BY FILLING IN
EACH SPACE WITH IMAGES OR WORDS THAT COME TO
MIND. LASTLY, REPEAT THE AFFIRMATION AT THE
BOTTOM OF THE PAGE OUT LOUD 3 TIMES.

My overall mood today:

calm	confident	nervous
happy	angry	grateful
sad	jealous	curious

Any others that came up:

My overall rating of the day:

1   2   3   4   5   6   7   8   9   10

Any and all other thoughts:

I RELEASE THIS DAY AND CALL BACK MY PEACE, POWER, AND POSITIVE ENERGY!

MY NIGHTLY
REFLECTION PROMPTS

READ THE PROMPTS BELOW AND RESPOND BY
FILLING IN EACH SPACE WITH IMAGES OR WORDS
THAT COME TO MIND.

The best things that
happened today:

Things I wish I could
change about today:

I am proud of myself
today because...

I think I still need
to work on...

MY NIGHTLY
REFLECTION PROMPTS

READ THE PROMPTS BELOW AND RESPOND BY FILLING IN
EACH SPACE WITH IMAGES OR WORDS THAT COME TO
MIND. LASTLY, REPEAT THE AFFIRMATION AT THE
BOTTOM OF THE PAGE OUT LOUD 3 TIMES.

My overall mood today:

calm   confident   nervous

happy   angry   grateful

sad   jealous   curious

Any others that came up:

My overall rating of the day:

1   2   3   4   5   6   7   8   9   10

Any and all other thoughts:

I RELEASE THIS DAY AND CALL BACK MY PEACE, POWER, AND POSITIVE ENERGY!

MY NIGHTLY
REFLECTION PROMPTS

READ THE PROMPTS BELOW AND RESPOND BY
FILLING IN EACH SPACE WITH IMAGES OR WORDS
THAT COME TO MIND.

The best things that
happened today:

Things I wish I could
change about today:

I am proud of myself
today because...

I think I still need
to work on...

MY NIGHTLY REFLECTION PROMPTS

READ THE PROMPTS BELOW AND RESPOND BY FILLING IN
EACH SPACE WITH IMAGES OR WORDS THAT COME TO
MIND. LASTLY, REPEAT THE AFFIRMATION AT THE
BOTTOM OF THE PAGE OUT LOUD 3 TIMES.

My overall mood today:

calm	confident	nervous
happy	angry	grateful
sad	jealous	curious

Any others that came up:

My overall rating of the day:

1   2   3   4   5   6   7   8   9   10

Any and all other thoughts:

I RELEASE THIS DAY AND CALL BACK MY PEACE, POWER, AND POSITIVE ENERGY!

MY NIGHTLY REFLECTION PROMPTS

READ THE PROMPTS BELOW AND RESPOND BY
FILLING IN EACH SPACE WITH IMAGES OR WORDS
THAT COME TO MIND.

The best things that
happened today:

Things I wish I could
change about today:

I am proud of myself
today because...

I think I still need
to work on...

MY NIGHTLY
REFLECTION PROMPTS

READ THE PROMPTS BELOW AND RESPOND BY FILLING IN
EACH SPACE WITH IMAGES OR WORDS THAT COME TO
MIND. LASTLY, REPEAT THE AFFIRMATION AT THE
BOTTOM OF THE PAGE OUT LOUD 3 TIMES.

My overall mood today:

calm	confident	nervous
happy	angry	grateful
sad	jealous	curious

Any others that came up:

My overall rating of the day:

1   2   3   4   5   6   7   8   9   10

Any and all other thoughts:

I RELEASE THIS DAY AND CALL BACK MY PEACE, POWER, AND POSITIVE ENERGY!

MY NIGHTLY REFLECTION PROMPTS

READ THE PROMPTS BELOW AND RESPOND BY
FILLING IN EACH SPACE WITH IMAGES OR WORDS
THAT COME TO MIND.

The best things that
happened today:

Things I wish I could
change about today:

I am proud of myself
today because...

I think I still need
to work on...

MY NIGHTLY REFLECTION PROMPTS

READ THE PROMPTS BELOW AND RESPOND BY FILLING IN
EACH SPACE WITH IMAGES OR WORDS THAT COME TO
MIND. LASTLY, REPEAT THE AFFIRMATION AT THE
BOTTOM OF THE PAGE OUT LOUD 3 TIMES.

My overall mood today:

calm   confident   nervous

happy   angry   grateful

sad   jealous   curious

Any others that came up:

My overall rating of the day:

1   2   3   4   5   6   7   8   9   10

Any and all other thoughts:

I RELEASE THIS DAY AND CALL BACK MY PEACE, POWER, AND POSITIVE ENERGY!

MY NIGHTLY
REFLECTION PROMPTS

READ THE PROMPTS BELOW AND RESPOND BY
FILLING IN EACH SPACE WITH IMAGES OR WORDS
THAT COME TO MIND.

The best things that
happened today:

Things I wish I could
change about today:

I am proud of myself
today because...

I think I still need
to work on...

MY NIGHTLY REFLECTION PROMPTS

READ THE PROMPTS BELOW AND RESPOND BY FILLING IN
EACH SPACE WITH IMAGES OR WORDS THAT COME TO
MIND. LASTLY, REPEAT THE AFFIRMATION AT THE
BOTTOM OF THE PAGE OUT LOUD 3 TIMES.

My overall mood today:

calm   confident   nervous

happy   angry   grateful

sad   jealous   curious

Any others that came up:

My overall rating of the day:

1   2   3   4   5   6   7   8   9   10

Any and all other thoughts:

I RELEASE THIS DAY AND CALL BACK MY PEACE, POWER, AND POSITIVE ENERGY!

MY NIGHTLY
REFLECTION PROMPTS

READ THE PROMPTS BELOW AND RESPOND BY
FILLING IN EACH SPACE WITH IMAGES OR WORDS
THAT COME TO MIND.

The best things that
happened today:

Things I wish I could
change about today:

I am proud of myself
today because...

I think I still need
to work on...

MY NIGHTLY
REFLECTION PROMPTS

READ THE PROMPTS BELOW AND RESPOND BY FILLING IN
EACH SPACE WITH IMAGES OR WORDS THAT COME TO
MIND. LASTLY, REPEAT THE AFFIRMATION AT THE
BOTTOM OF THE PAGE OUT LOUD 3 TIMES.

My overall mood today:

calm	confident	nervous
happy	angry	grateful
sad	jealous	curious

Any others that came up:

My overall rating of the day:

1   2   3   4   5   6   7   8   9   10

Any and all other thoughts:

I RELEASE THIS DAY AND CALL BACK MY PEACE, POWER, AND POSITIVE ENERGY!

MY NIGHTLY
REFLECTION PROMPTS

READ THE PROMPTS BELOW AND RESPOND BY
FILLING IN EACH SPACE WITH IMAGES OR WORDS
THAT COME TO MIND.

The best things that
happened today:

Things I wish I could
change about today:

I am proud of myself
today because...

I think I still need
to work on...

MY NIGHTLY
REFLECTION PROMPTS

READ THE PROMPTS BELOW AND RESPOND BY FILLING IN
EACH SPACE WITH IMAGES OR WORDS THAT COME TO
MIND. LASTLY, REPEAT THE AFFIRMATION AT THE
BOTTOM OF THE PAGE OUT LOUD 3 TIMES.

My overall mood today:

calm	confident	nervous
happy	angry	grateful
sad	jealous	curious

Any others that came up:

My overall rating of the day:

1   2   3   4   5   6   7   8   9   10

Any and all other thoughts:

I RELEASE THIS DAY AND CALL BACK MY PEACE, POWER, AND POSITIVE ENERGY!

MY NIGHTLY REFLECTION PROMPTS

READ THE PROMPTS BELOW AND RESPOND BY
FILLING IN EACH SPACE WITH IMAGES OR WORDS
THAT COME TO MIND.

The best things that
happened today:

Things I wish I could
change about today:

I am proud of myself
today because...

I think I still need
to work on...

MY NIGHTLY REFLECTION PROMPTS

READ THE PROMPTS BELOW AND RESPOND BY FILLING IN
EACH SPACE WITH IMAGES OR WORDS THAT COME TO
MIND. LASTLY, REPEAT THE AFFIRMATION AT THE
BOTTOM OF THE PAGE OUT LOUD 3 TIMES.

My overall mood today:

calm   confident   nervous

happy   angry   grateful

sad   jealous   curious

Any others that came up:

My overall rating of the day:

1   2   3   4   5   6   7   8   9   10

Any and all other thoughts:

I RELEASE THIS DAY AND CALL BACK MY PEACE, POWER, AND POSITIVE ENERGY!

MY NIGHTLY REFLECTION PROMPTS

READ THE PROMPTS BELOW AND RESPOND BY
FILLING IN EACH SPACE WITH IMAGES OR WORDS
THAT COME TO MIND.

The best things that
happened today:

Things I wish I could
change about today:

I am proud of myself
today because...

I think I still need
to work on...

MY NIGHTLY REFLECTION PROMPTS

READ THE PROMPTS BELOW AND RESPOND BY FILLING IN
EACH SPACE WITH IMAGES OR WORDS THAT COME TO
MIND. LASTLY, REPEAT THE AFFIRMATION AT THE
BOTTOM OF THE PAGE OUT LOUD 3 TIMES.

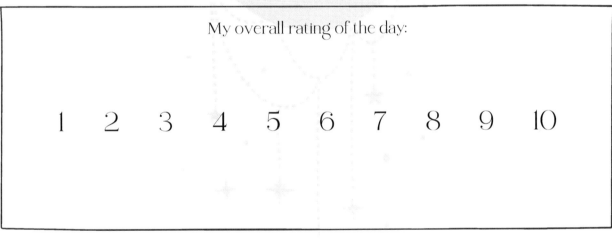

My overall mood today:

calm	confident	nervous
happy	angry	grateful
sad	jealous	curious

Any others that came up:

My overall rating of the day:

1   2   3   4   5   6   7   8   9   10

Any and all other thoughts:

I RELEASE THIS DAY AND CALL BACK MY PEACE, POWER, AND POSITIVE ENERGY!

MY NIGHTLY REFLECTION PROMPTS

READ THE PROMPTS BELOW AND RESPOND BY
FILLING IN EACH SPACE WITH IMAGES OR WORDS
THAT COME TO MIND.

The best things that
happened today:

Things I wish I could
change about today:

I am proud of myself
today because...

I think I still need
to work on...

MY NIGHTLY REFLECTION PROMPTS

READ THE PROMPTS BELOW AND RESPOND BY FILLING IN
EACH SPACE WITH IMAGES OR WORDS THAT COME TO
MIND. LASTLY, REPEAT THE AFFIRMATION AT THE
BOTTOM OF THE PAGE OUT LOUD 3 TIMES.

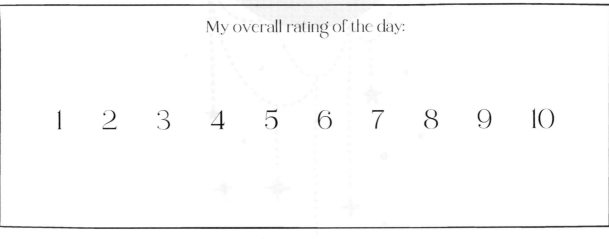

My overall mood today:

calm	confident	nervous
happy	angry	grateful
sad	jealous	curious

Any others that came up:

My overall rating of the day:

1   2   3   4   5   6   7   8   9   10

Any and all other thoughts:

I RELEASE THIS DAY AND CALL BACK MY PEACE, POWER, AND POSITIVE ENERGY!

MY NIGHTLY
REFLECTION PROMPTS

READ THE PROMPTS BELOW AND RESPOND BY
FILLING IN EACH SPACE WITH IMAGES OR WORDS
THAT COME TO MIND.

The best things that
happened today:

Things I wish I could
change about today:

I am proud of myself
today because...

I think I still need
to work on...

MY NIGHTLY
REFLECTION PROMPTS

READ THE PROMPTS BELOW AND RESPOND BY FILLING IN
EACH SPACE WITH IMAGES OR WORDS THAT COME TO
MIND. LASTLY, REPEAT THE AFFIRMATION AT THE
BOTTOM OF THE PAGE OUT LOUD 3 TIMES.

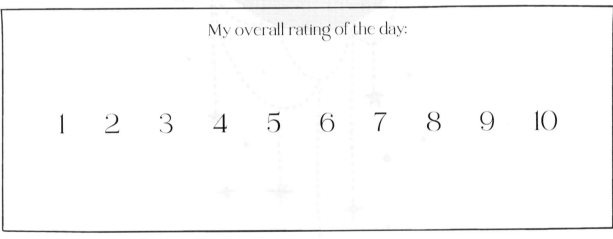

My overall mood today:

calm	confident	nervous
happy	angry	grateful
sad	jealous	curious

Any others that came up:

My overall rating of the day:

1   2   3   4   5   6   7   8   9   10

Any and all other thoughts:

I RELEASE THIS DAY AND CALL BACK MY PEACE, POWER, AND POSITIVE ENERGY!

MY NIGHTLY REFLECTION PROMPTS

READ THE PROMPTS BELOW AND RESPOND BY
FILLING IN EACH SPACE WITH IMAGES OR WORDS
THAT COME TO MIND.

The best things that
happened today:

Things I wish I could
change about today:

I am proud of myself
today because...

I think I still need
to work on...

MY NIGHTLY
REFLECTION PROMPTS

READ THE PROMPTS BELOW AND RESPOND BY FILLING IN
EACH SPACE WITH IMAGES OR WORDS THAT COME TO
MIND. LASTLY, REPEAT THE AFFIRMATION AT THE
BOTTOM OF THE PAGE OUT LOUD 3 TIMES.

My overall mood today:

calm	confident	nervous
happy	angry	grateful
sad	jealous	curious

Any others that came up:

My overall rating of the day:

1   2   3   4   5   6   7   8   9   10

Any and all other thoughts:

I RELEASE THIS DAY AND CALL BACK MY PEACE, POWER, AND POSITIVE ENERGY!

MY NIGHTLY
REFLECTION PROMPTS

READ THE PROMPTS BELOW AND RESPOND BY
FILLING IN EACH SPACE WITH IMAGES OR WORDS
THAT COME TO MIND.

The best things that
happened today:

Things I wish I could
change about today:

I am proud of myself
today because...

I think I still need
to work on...

MY NIGHTLY
REFLECTION PROMPTS

READ THE PROMPTS BELOW AND RESPOND BY FILLING IN
EACH SPACE WITH IMAGES OR WORDS THAT COME TO
MIND. LASTLY, REPEAT THE AFFIRMATION AT THE
BOTTOM OF THE PAGE OUT LOUD 3 TIMES.

My overall mood today:

calm	confident	nervous
happy	angry	grateful
sad	jealous	curious

Any others that came up:

My overall rating of the day:

1   2   3   4   5   6   7   8   9   10

Any and all other thoughts:

I RELEASE THIS DAY AND CALL BACK MY PEACE, POWER, AND POSITIVE ENERGY!

MY NIGHTLY REFLECTION PROMPTS

READ THE PROMPTS BELOW AND RESPOND BY
FILLING IN EACH SPACE WITH IMAGES OR WORDS
THAT COME TO MIND.

The best things that
happened today:

Things I wish I could
change about today:

I am proud of myself
today because...

I think I still need
to work on...

MY NIGHTLY
REFLECTION PROMPTS

READ THE PROMPTS BELOW AND RESPOND BY FILLING IN
EACH SPACE WITH IMAGES OR WORDS THAT COME TO
MIND. LASTLY, REPEAT THE AFFIRMATION AT THE
BOTTOM OF THE PAGE OUT LOUD 3 TIMES.

My overall mood today:

calm	confident	nervous
happy	angry	grateful
sad	jealous	curious

Any others that came up:

My overall rating of the day:

1   2   3   4   5   6   7   8   9   10

Any and all other thoughts:

I RELEASE THIS DAY AND CALL BACK MY PEACE, POWER, AND POSITIVE ENERGY!

MY NIGHTLY
REFLECTION PROMPTS

READ THE PROMPTS BELOW AND RESPOND BY
FILLING IN EACH SPACE WITH IMAGES OR WORDS
THAT COME TO MIND.

The best things that
happened today:

Things I wish I could
change about today:

I am proud of myself
today because...

I think I still need
to work on...

MY NIGHTLY
REFLECTION PROMPTS

READ THE PROMPTS BELOW AND RESPOND BY FILLING IN
EACH SPACE WITH IMAGES OR WORDS THAT COME TO
MIND. LASTLY, REPEAT THE AFFIRMATION AT THE
BOTTOM OF THE PAGE OUT LOUD 3 TIMES.

My overall mood today:

calm	confident	nervous
happy	angry	grateful
sad	jealous	curious

Any others that came up:

My overall rating of the day:

1 2 3 4 5 6 7 8 9 10

Any and all other thoughts:

I RELEASE THIS DAY AND CALL BACK MY PEACE, POWER, AND POSITIVE ENERGY!

Made in the USA
Las Vegas, NV
01 October 2023

78455290R00101